ZEN AND THE ART OF
MULTIPLE SCLEROSIS

ZEN AND THE ART OF MULTIPLE SCLEROSIS

Jeff Pinney

**Edited and with a Foreword
by Douglas Smith PhD**

iUniverse, Inc.
Bloomington

Zen and the Art of Multiple Sclerosis

iUniverse books may be ordered through booksellers or by contacting:

iUniverse
1663 Liberty Drive
Bloomington, IN 47403
www.iuniverse.com
1-800-Authors (1-800-288-4677)

Because of the dynamic nature of the Internet, any web addresses or links contained in this book may have changed since publication and may no longer be valid. The views expressed in this work are solely those of the author and do not necessarily reflect the views of the publisher, and the publisher hereby disclaims any responsibility for them.

Any people depicted in stock imagery provided by Thinkstock are models, and such images are being used for illustrative purposes only.

Certain stock imagery © Thinkstock.

ISBN: 978-1-4759-3456-4 (sc)
ISBN: 978-1-4759-3457-1 (e)

Library of Congress Control Number: 2012911387

Printed in the United States of America

iUniverse rev. date: 07/13/2012

To Shirley Rose

1956 – 2010

Contents

Foreword

Douglas Smith PhD

We are very familiar with the kind of hero's journey that traverses the vale of despond to reach the summit of achievement after many trials and tribulations. Less familiar are those equally heroic journeys which begin high on a mountainside only to descend under the tug of gravity towards the somber regions below. These are the stories of promethean souls who, though afflicted with chronic degenerative disease, succeed in bringing light to the world.

Jeff Pinney, afflicted with multiple sclerosis for thirty-five years, is one of those promethean souls whom I am proud to claim as a friend. We first met about eight years ago, when Jeff was living "on the Buckslide" and I was serving as a hospice worker. My task was to visit with people who were house-bound for reasons of illness or grief. Jeff was confined to a wheelchair by then, so I entered his home without expecting him to greet me at the door. From the vestibule I could see that an electric lift had been installed on the stairwell to provide access to the second-floor. My gaze wandered over the massive wooden beams towards the wall on my left, where some oil paintings were hung. These were renderings of nature, a subject common enough in Haliburton; yet they glowed with profound artistry in their courageous delving into shadow, their devotion to detail, and their loving evocation of snow.

The world looks very different when you're caged in a wheelchair every waking hour of the day. In spite of all the benefits which technology has conferred, enhancing comfort and mobility, for someone afflicted with multiple sclerosis the situation is one of steadily diminishing competence. How does one in a state of debility face the world as a spiritual warrior? The Zen of it is to keep on your toes even when your legs are long gone. Knowing that information is power, you learn not to squander your remaining assets, even though it is tempting to engage an abled stranger by divulging your private affairs. To preserve a last shred of dignity you keep some precious memories to yourself.

With Jeff's persmission I will lift the curtain just a bit on one area of his life into which I intruded, quite literally. This concerns his achievement as an underground horticulturalist.

Jeff had left his home on the Buckslide and taken up residence in the town of Minden. One cold day in February

2006, I dropped by his new place, again in my role as a hospice worker. The television was crackling with bad news and we took a few minutes getting comfortable with each other by denouncing the current crop of politicians. Then Jeff asked me if I would do him a favour. There had been some ice buildup around the door of the garden shed, and he wondered if I might chop it away in order for him to get access to some equipment inside.

I did so. Then I put my shoulder to the door, but it didn't budge. On the second attempt I could feel it start to give. Unaware that I was playing out an old Marx brothers gag, I put full force to it the third time, which sent me sailing over the threshold from wintry chill into a tropical paradise. Everywhere there were pot plants shooting up like buoyant green fountains. The plants were set in hydroponic tubs where circulating waters gurgled lullingly. The hooded grow-lux bulbs were set on low to mimic September sunlight. Dense with moisture, the air was heavily perfumed.

Right away I began to sweat, so I took off my coat and waited for Jeff to arrive. Gliding around in his wheelchair, Jeff showed me the workbench where he did his cross-breeding experiments. He traced out the piping and pointed to the valves that regulated the water flow. Enthusiastically he explained the ratio of nutrients that percolated amongst the root systems. Still consumed by wonderment, I had trouble following the technical side of his discourse; but I gathered that Jeff had succeeded in crossing the Northern Lights and White Rhino strains to produce a cannabis hybrid that showed great promise in relieving the muscular spasms which torment MS patients.

Next thing I heard, Jeff had been busted. His policy as a healing horticulturalist was never to sell what he grew, so it must have been a local busybody who alerted the cops. Driving by Jeff's home, I could see from the road that the shed door was sealed with a lock and chain. It was not my worry that Jeff would endure prison time. Under the verdict of multiple sclerosis he was serving a life sentence already.

Who would feel genuine gratitude when given sanctuary in the house of the dying? In reading Jeff's account you will occasionally sense his bitterness at the way things have turned out. Over the years one expressive function after another has been erased: his ability to make love, to build things, to target-shoot, to carve, to paint, and now to write. He lives these days amongst the moribundi in a long-term care facility. With an intensity of feeling I can scarcely imagine he asks the question which every seer propounds: When everything is taken away, what is left?

In writing this book Jeff Pinney, an enfeebled Prometheus, has broken the chains binding him to that baneful rock, his battery-powered chair.

Ten Thousand Little Cuts

An old man sleeps with his conscience at night
Young kids sleep with their dreams
While the mentally ill sit perfectly still
And live through life's in-betweens

John Prine, "The Late John Garfield Blues"

This tale is dedicated, first, to all those personal support workers who have cared for me during my advanced stage of multiple sclerosis. Regrettably, many of the dearest ones have since retired, while some of their younger replacements appear only to exercise tolerance towards me.

I also dedicate this writing to Shirley Rose Patterson, my late confidante and companion, who provided constant encouragment while I wrote this book. I didn't get to know all that much about Shirley in this life, but we must have been an item in past lives, as we were totally comfortable being in each other's presence. Between us there was nothing left to say, nothing to do, apart from just being together.

I would also like to honour my advocates Eric and Carolynn, without whom this writing would not have happened. Carolynn has kept her good humour while straightening out my tangled affairs, while Eric has cheerfully unjammed my computer more times than I can count.

I am presently 65 years old and have lived with slow, progressive multiple sclerosis for more than half that time. Some readers may recognize the title of this story as an allusion to Robert Pirsig's *Zen and the Art of Motorcycle Maintenance*. These same readers may think that years of suffering multiple sclerosis bear no relation to fixing a motorcycle. But likely they have never tried to start a 1965 Harley Davidson Sportster with an automatic spark advance. Even that beautiful bike could not make me truly happy. Yet even after so many years with MS, I am happy much of the time, and I'm still ticking over. Had I been working on that motorcycle in full health for the past three decades, I would not necessarily be any the happier. And I'm pretty sure that Harley wouldn't be running much anymore.

I have read that Tibetan monks voluntarily live in cramped cells in their search for enlightenment. They enter monasteries to find inner peace, harmony and eternal bliss. They give up everything to gain everything. MS, with its 10,000 myelin cuts, has stripped away everything I thought was important to me. MS brings on death in slow motion, exposing my withering on a day-by-day basis. The constant fatigue which is the hallmark of MS is a continual reminder of how much it takes away. It robs all my strength and mobility like a nightmare that begins at dawn and never lets up. It takes my aspirations, my independence, my hopes and dreams. It takes each day and Sunday, too. It doesn't go on holiday. It settles in like a mortgage and never goes away.

I can piss and moan about it, or I can regard this unrelenting affliction as my life-long teacher. I am free to make that choice. By writing this book I hope in the first place to distill a few lessons that may assist those who suffer from chronic disease or physical impairment. As for the rest who are still abled and carefree it may come as a shock to learn that one day they too will die. This is an unhappy truth which sick folk must accept as the price of their existence. It is hard to pretend otherwise. So I wonder: if I stare in the mirror long enough, looking fixedly at death, will I vanquish the illusion that makes me grasp for shiny things with a shrivelled hand?

Searching for the Cure

You can waste your time sitting in the waiting rooms of doctors' offices. The more you do that, the more opinions you will get. You can spend thousands flying from country to country seeking a miracle cure. All you get is unhappiness, because now, as well as having MS, you're broke and your hopes are dashed. My opinion is that MS has its own reality and that it marches along to its own drummer. It doesn't matter if you pump iron, do crawdads around on your back in a swimming pool three times a week, drink hundred-year old scotch, snort wheat grass, smoke righteous weed, or pray to the Grandfaloons of your choosing. MS is going to do what MS is going to do, regardless.

By the by, when the great humanitarian Mark Emery surveyed the world for consensus on what was the ultimate pot—and by this he didn't mean just the most powerful—he was led to Gypsy Joe's Tripping Weed, which magically alleviated many of the grievous problems besetting humanity, including robot routine, squelched creativity and general lustrelessness. Problem is, Gypsy Joe's Tripping Weed is only found on Sumatra, an emerald isle long distant from Minden Ontario, where my wrecked frame is currently deposited.

There is one possibility that may hold promise. I have read that scientists are genetically altering pigs, so that pig tissues can be substituted for dysfunctional human body parts. Since my whole body is basically toast, I could arrange to have my precious head transplanted onto a pig's body. Might work! Turn me loose in a corn field and I'll snuffle around like some mutant centaur.

Yippie yi yo kayah. Oink.

Pardon me, but before I start my story I have a rant to voice! Of course you can disregard the rant and move on to the story itself. But here it goes anyway. At the dentist's office I read in the Readers Digest that some distinguished chap published an article in a scientific medical journal claiming that, following diagnosis, most of the progression of MS is just psychosomatic. Psychosomatic! Now there's a word that really boils my potatoes. This theory claims that most of the suffering I experience is concocted in my head. Well, hello, if it isn't in my head, where is it experienced? Wherever else it may be, I frankly don't know or care.

Does psychosomatic mean that much of the pain and suffering I am experiencing is an illusion? Everything in the past is memory, and everything in the future is speculation. These too are illusions. Memories are fickle and we can only make guesses about the unknown future. The one thing that's completely reliable is this present instant, this thin slice of actuality which is constantly shifting from imagination to memory. So by that measure most of our lives are lived in illusion, psychosomatically.

Whether I think I have MS or I know I have MS, I still can't walk. So, Doctor Potato Head, what's the cure for my illusion?

Jesse was a Shooter

For the sake of a good story call me Jesse. Jesse thought he was a shooter, an adept marksman with a steady hand and a sure tread. He fancied smooth-bore rifles from the buffalo days. Jesse thought he was a lot of things until MS stripped them away. Though he would mourn the loss of many years, eventually Jesse realized those years were a product of ego, and he tried dropping them, years and ego both, like a bad habit. I use the name Jesse because my great-grandfather met Jesse James, the outlaw. When asked about this notorious killer, my grandfather said, "I don't know anything about the things he did. All I know is the man I met was a gentleman." So I use the name Jesse in reference to an elusive gentleman, as a reminder not to act like a common bandit.

As a teenager back in the 50's I was into trap shooting and long-range target shooting. I collected two of the rifles Jesse James, the outlaw, would have used, a Henry and a Sharps. Jesse used the Sharps as a long gun, and though I hadn't fired this gun in years, I would use it, as you will see, to protect myself later in life.

I will tell my story because I am a storyteller confined to a wheelchair, burdened with time. It will be a funny story because I am ordinarily a funny guy. The facts and dates may not be precise; it's the story that counts. This story is true to the best of my recollection, yet I would never let the truth get in the way of a good joke. This story is my gift to all those brothers and sisters who have multiple sclerosis and to anyone else who finds themselves hopelessly caught up in the thickness of thin things. I am hoping that in telling my story we together can experience some relief from this ridiculous and crushing illness, that we together can find a degree of happiness, if not actually enjoy a few laughs.

I have now had slow progressive MS for 35 years. It is not important what that has done to me physically. What is important is how I dealt with it mentally. Looking back, my journey seems funny, though it was not so at the time. It is said "the road to enlightenment passes through hell." It is not a road I would have taken by choice. Very few are those who do. Learning to travel that hard road is at the heart of my story.

At the onset of the disease I did not know my own mind. Knowing I had MS (though there were very few physical symptoms at onset), my life decisions were driven by what I thought was coming, not by what was actually here in the moment. Knowing I had MS locked me out of the future, but it also locked me out of the past. If I was to be happy, I would have to learn to live in the moment, where life and spontaneity reside. Being diagnosed with MS firmly planted my feet on that enlightening road which leads through hell to a big belly laugh.

My first major decision, which sets the stage for this story, was that I would not share my approaching impairment with any of the friends I had accumulated around me. When my condition finally became obvious, I intended to gather up my bag of misery like a thief in the night and disappear to parts unknown. To make this plan a little more palatable, I decided I would take my then girlfriend along with me. From her I hid my deep fear that I would gradually degenerate from my present attractive, virile self into a smashed bag of hammers. I was afraid to present her with that future eventuality.

Instead, I buried my fears beneath a long term future plan so brilliant in its conception that she would not see how much fear was a part of its construction. This would be a relationship built upon a rock solid foundation, alright! One based above all in truth and honesty, though admittedly these were virtues that had to be deferred for the time being. Deferred at least until she loved me enough through long-term familiarity, or until I had moved her so far out in the boonies that there would be nowhere else to go. That place for me was the "bush" of northern Ontario, where you could talk to the animals and be heard.

Looking back, now that my body is that smashed bag of hammers, I don't think my intentions were truly malicious. I can forgive myself, as I know I truly loved her, as I love all sentient beings. But at the time I was shy, desperate, scared, lonely and without a doubt insane.

Over the years I have tried to match my insanity to the insanity of the disease I am living with. I disagree with the opinion that people with MS are simply normal people who have a permanent disability. I for one am completely bonkers. Not necessarily unhappy or unlovable, just crazy.

But getting back to the girl I planned to hoodwink so long ago. She was no fool. She jumped ship in 1988 just before I sailed off to Yoyoville. Was her hair auburn, blonde, or black? It was not red, that much I remember.

I was never really comfortable around women. My father taught me to respect the ladies, take your hat off and open the door, but I just took that to mean you should believe every word they said. Though I loved them at a distance, I just didn't do well talking with them. I never learned the skills of saying one thing when your intent is something else, which is an aspect of communication that women seemed to have developed very well.

As an example, while living homeless in Nassau in the Bahamas, I daydreamed how nice it would be to meet a pretty girl who would invite me to come and stay with her awhile. One day, as I was walking along, a pretty girl actually dropped a pair of panties on me from the first floor balcony of the British Colonial Hotel. She called down, asking if I might retrieve them for her. Instead of taking them up to her apartment and introducing myself, I put a stone in them for weight and threw them up for her to catch. As you can see, I was hopeless as a suitor.

I didn't feel comfortable around men much either. Though I had male friends, most were acquaintances I didn't much care for. I didn't mind some of them as individuals, but in groups or clubs I found them to be infantile, boring and dangerous. Still do, for that matter! As individuals we males appear to be more dangerous to women then to each other.

I had been pretty much going the way the wind blows since I was fourteen, two years in the Bahamas, a year in Mexico, five years on the east coast of Canada, five on the west coast.

Deeper even than my need to bond with someone was a main driving force pushing me to get where I felt closest to home, so I could process some of the bad news that was coming my way. What I really needed was a place just to rest. I had the nagging feeling that events were moving so fast that the important things in life were slipping past. Brief encounters that didn't go anywhere were my daily fare. With my inner nervousness I was creating bad karma for myself which I would have to deal with sooner or later.

My life at that time was unstable and chaotic to say the least. After living rurally for most of my life, I ended up bunking on Crawford Avenue in downtown Toronto with a girl I met in the rocky mountains near Jasper Alberta. (Another thing about me and women, I always found it easier to communicate with them in the presence of nature's glory.) So between the oo's and ah's of wonder I obtained Brenda's phone number in Toronto. A couple of years later, after delivering a car from Prince George, British Columbia, to Toronto, I called her up. We renewed our oo's and ah's, and soon I found myself living with her.

Things were not going well. Having been raised in a time when it was unacceptable to instill discipline by beating children black and blue, I lacked the mental discipline either to learn a useful trade or take training as an artist. As I became older, I began to pay the price of my undisciplined life. The only work I could get in Toronto was manual labour at day agencies, traveling around the city on public transportation doing various humdrum jobs in different locations, often in the odious suburbs.

On the other hand, Brenda, my room-mate, worked at a trendy advertising agency. On Fridays Brenda and the staff she worked with would leave work at noon and meet at their favourite drinking establishment. After a few good rounds, Brenda would return to the apartment a couple of hours before I did. Usually she would bring an additional bottle of wine with her. She didn't like to drink alone, but what the hell, it was the end of the week. TGIF! By the time I got home Brenda would have concluded that the main reason for all her problems in life was the fact that I was living in her apartment. By the time I got home she would have thrown all my clothes out the window, and I would have to go about retrieving my scattered duds from the front lawn.

Back then I didn't know much about how relationships were supposed to work, but I did sense that this wasn't quite it. Sure, I hoped we could fix it with time; but time was something I didn't have, as my body might start to turn all crikum-crankum before I was ready (as if we are ever ready). So I planned to defer our problems with the theory that the only way to find what we really wanted in life was to live in a place where you didn't have to pay rent or mortgage, since by doing either you didn't have time left to figure out what you really wanted in life.

For once Brenda agreed. So it was decided that I would move to Oakville where my father lived. There I would start a painting business to earn the money to buy the house to live in the country where we would find eternal bliss and happiness. Brenda loved the idea. Why not? She didn't really have to do anything and her main issue in life, at least when drinking, would be solved.

There was just one little problem with my plan: To find peace and happiness by changing locations I had to take my whole slovenly self along.

The English Painter

The reason I chose the painting business was I had always been a good artist by nature. I simply didn't have the discipline to turn a parlour trick used to justify goofing off into a productive skill. That would come later. For the time being I turned my native talent into (as wage-earning painters say) cutting a clean edge with semi-gloss. My dad had been a painter and he knew all the old-school tricks of the trade. Oakville was at the time one of the wealthiest per capita towns in Canada, so it was a good location to start a service business.

I began working for a contractor whose hook was to advertise himself as an "English painter". Oakville at that time was a conservative, waspish, predominantly old English town, well on its way to becoming a dormitory suburb of Toronto. When people there needed a painter they were thrilled to hire a posh English painter to beautify their tacky columned manors and semi-detached bungalows.

The problem was this guy couldn't paint worth spit. Or rather, he had the skill, but he was the kind of boss who was always trying to cram ten pounds of shit into a five pound bag. He tried to cut corners, but as a house-painter he wasn't good enough to know what corners you could cut. Needless to say it was only a matter of time until he created a disaster, a really big disaster, a disaster so big he was sued for forty thousand dollars. Since he wasn't a citizen of Canada he split back to England. I had tried to warn him that my dad saw it coming. I told him my uncle, who worked for Pittsburgh paints, saw the mistake. But the English painter wouldn't listen to advice. Now he had flown the coop on a one-way ticket.

For the time being Brenda had faded from the picture, so I moved in with the girl whom the English Painter left behind in Oakville. I cultivated an English accent, started calling other tradesmen "old chap", and in no time became the English Painter myself.

After running a successful painting and wall papering business in Oakville for three years, visiting Brenda in Toronto on occasion (sly dog that I was), I found myself running way too fast for my own good. I had been diagnosed with MS twelve years ago, in 1976, and the physical symptoms were now starting to appear, as well as bladder incontinence for which I required self-catheterization. I had developed occasional foot-drop, a common symptom of MS, in which your foot slumps to the ground in mid-stride. I could compensate these symptoms, as I was still physically very strong, but my mental state and life-stye were deteriorating. In the back of my mind I held onto my ultimate intention of finding a place where I could devote time to my health and spiritual well-being. Yet presently I was going in the opposite direction. The karma I was creating was affecting my current state, and already the MS was nipping at my heels.

At last disaster struck. I was standing near the top of a twenty-foot extension ladder, which was balanced on top of a ten-foot square of scaffolding, painting the peak of a two-story house. I was actually spraying a hornets' nest with wasp blaster when I fell off. I was air-borne ever so briefly until I hit the scaffolding twenty feet below, breaking my wrist. I would have to spend six weeks with a cast on my wrist, all stressed out because I had so many contracts to finish. In my frenzied work-style I too had become the English Painter.

It was because of this break—to my wrist and from my work—that I found what I imagined would be my Shangri-la, an opportunity that would change my life dramatically over the next twelve years.

On the Buckslide

During my period of convalescence I took a trip north to cottage country. I chose the Haliburton Highlands because my fondest childhood days were spent there, swimming and playing with my older sister. My family vacationed two weeks a year from about 1952 to 1960. As a kid this was where I had truly bonded with nature, experiencing feelings of comfort and belonging that remain to this day.

I drove two hundred miles to the town of Minden, stopping at the Rockcliffe Hotel in all its fabled grunginess for lunch. There I read the local real-estate publications. Real estate in the mid 1980's was high, as were interest rates, and I pretty much had resigned myself to the fact that I would have to find a piece of property in the bush, hopefully on or near water. I intended to put a tent or trailer on the site, and then build a house from scratch.

While contemplating this grim prospect and imagining what it would entail, my attention alighted on a small for sale notice in the Minden Times. What caught my attention was the offer of a three-season dwelling on the Buckslide Road, within walking distance of Halls Lake and Highway 35. I knew exactly where that was. The cottage my parents rented so long ago was on Halls Lake, and as a small boy I had spent much of my time observing nature in and around the streams and beaver dams that ran alongside that very road.

Halls Lake lay north of Carnarvon, a twenty minute drive from Minden. Carnarvon I remembered as a crossroads settlement with a population of about thirty-five, including a dog with an infected ear. If you ever should find yourself in Carnarvon, you could assume you were lost. As I drove once again through Carnarvon I reflected on how much I preferred the name Buckslide Road as a place to live, compared to the pompous road and street names in and around suburban Toronto, where the upwardly mobile puffed themselves up with snotty-sounding names like Don Mills and Agincourt. I, on the other hand, could backslide with the best of them on the Buckslide. As someone looking to drop out of society, the name already had real appeal.

Nearing Halls Lake, I was already overwhelmed by the familiar smell of the northern pine forests and the vista of inviting lakes. Here was the authentic atmosphere of nature that vanishes the closer you approach the cities. If the development boom continued in high gear, a few decades from now this rural paradise would also be consumed. As Halls Lake came into view I pulled my van over on the side. There was a turnaround at the end of Buckslide Road near the lakeshore. It was just as I remembered it. The lake, about a mile square, was very blue. I knew it was one of the deepest and cleanest lakes in the region. I could see the roof of the cottage my parents rented so long ago, about five hundred yards up the highway, near the beach where my sister and I used to swim for hours each day. The part which really transported me back in time was a lagoon on the opposite side of the road from the lake. It was formed by a stream which in turn was formed by the overflow of a very large beaver dam. The stream, the lagoon, and the remains of an old abandoned cottage were completely hidden from view by an impenetrable mass of bull rushes, swamp grass, thornbush, alders, nettles, day lilies and Joe Pye weed. Impenetrable to all but a five year old boy and his memory, who knew that it was all still there to be experienced.

I followed the stream along the Buckslide Road. I couldn't actually see the stream, though I could tell where it was running under the lush vegetation. One hundred yards along the road the stream ended at a beaver dam. The dam was a large one, about two hundred yards long. Beyond the dam was open water. The open water ran along beside the right side of the road about three hundred yards, then disappeared behind trees and dense brush, I could see that it extended much farther, ending in bull rushes and a large beaver meadow beyond. The open water before me was about five hundred yards across. There was white pine, maple, beach, spruce, basswood and birch forest on the other side, and I could see at about midpoint that the land narrowed to a thin row of cedar trees with open water beyond. (I found out later that there were actually three more beaver ponds beyond this point.) I continued another two hundred yards up the road and came to the real estate sign, marking the property I was looking for.

The dwelling was actually a large two-story duck & deer hunting camp. Although it was situated only fifty feet from the road, the area around it was so completely taken over by bush that you could hardly see the building for the trees. It would be a struggle just to get through to the front door, if indeed it had one. This place had not been inhabited by anything other than chipmunks and racoons for a very long time. I had to fight my way through alder shrub, thorn bushes and bramble until I came to the front of the building. I looked down along the side. The trees and dense underbrush grew right up to the walls. The poplars were even bending over the roof to attain the sunlight afforded by the building space.

The land fell sharply away from the road to the back of the house, but I was determined to get through the thorn bush, the thistles, the prickly bushes, the vines, the grab-you trees, the snags, in order to get to the back of the building. Part way there, I almost fell in the dug well, which was completely grown over.

I continued on, ripping and tearing through the undergrowth. I was really starting to get into this. Somehow the confusion and tangle of nature around me matched the anxiety, depression, and guilt that infested my mind. I reached the back of the house. The block foundation rose ten feet above the ground line. There was a ten foot overhang, with the house rising a story and a half above that. The whole building was covered with particle board painted purple, which is the colour you get by mixing together all the half-used cans of paint left over in the garage.

There were no window-panes anywhere. Where they may once have been, screening was tacked over square or oblong openings. The limb of a large cherry tree grew right through one of these windows, setting leaves inside the house itself. On the downside, this would be a place that would be hard to heat. Upside, firewood was not far way. But none of this was what concerned me at the moment. Judging from what I had seen while driving up the road, the beaver meadow must be somewhere close behind this house, and I needed to find it fast. My exploration had become urgent, because I was being eaten alive by black flies.

I continued on, but if anything the ripping, pulling, tearing, clinging bush became even denser, until I tore around like a whirling dervish and spun into a new reality. It was incredible. Suddenly I was standing in a calm, peaceful meadow. In front of me was a panorama of lush green grasses rimmed by forest. It seemed as if the place existed in a separate reality from everything around. It was hot. A low hum of heat bugs, but no black flies. Some activity of small birds here and there, doing their own thing. The sense of peacefulness pervaded everything, as if the meadow existed in a different time and space.

I was overwhelmed with the peacefulness of my surroundings. My mind settled into serenity while I observed my surroundings in awe. My previous goals melted away. I was no longer trying to get somewhere. Now I was in reality. This place seemed timeless. I was experiencing the stillness, the tranquillity of mind, which I had lost sometime in my childhood. For me this was a brief rush, yet it provided me with unshakeable motivation.

When I turned around and looked back at the house my previous grasping, goal-driven mind returned. I recognized that if I cleared the trees and bush between the house and meadow and built a large open porch along the back of the house, I could simply step out onto the platform and have all this to myself. I could own this feeling, ready to sample whenever I opened the back door.

Like everyone else, I had been raised and trained within the most powerful brainwashing machine ever devised in the history of mankind. To date, the American empire, together with its advertising media, had convinced an entire society to believe that if you want something then you must own it. As a conditioned product of this mighty machine, I desired to possess this place, so that I could experience my current ungraspable state whenever I wanted. We have allowed this kind of thinking to take over our minds like a bloom of mildew on a damp pillow. Such attitudes are what made our country the great nation it is, an impressive edifice built on impermanence.

Suddenly the strangest sound I had ever heard issued from the beaver meadow. I turned around, all else forgotten.

What was that sound? I looked and looked. Everything was the same. Nothing moved. And then I heard it again. What *is* that? I couldn't tell if it was close or far. It sounded like a bowling ball being dropped in a pond. I looked again but couldn't see anything. I started back. Nature itself had called but I didn't know the code. Jerked out of my stale mind into the blazing moment—nature can do that so well!

Reflecting on that mystery at a later time, I realized that what I had heard was a Least Bittern, reputed to be the most camouflaged bird in North America. Few people have ever seen one. Like so many of my favourite birds, like so many frog species, the Least Bittern faces extinction.

Thrashing through the bush, heading for the road, I decided then and there to get the phone number of the real-estate company from the road-side sign, to call them and make an offer while I was still up and functioning.

Wow, the black flies are sure waiting for me. Given the condition of this place, mine is likely to be the only offer. Damn, I just ran into the well again! At least the place has a roof, so I can stay out of the rain while I fix it up. Hey, wait a minute. There's a truck in front. That means somebody's inside.

I went in to introduce myself and look around. The front door opened onto what I presumed was once the kitchen. There was no running water or cupboards of any description. The first room opened at each end into a large living area. There were two men dressed like painters preparing to blow stucco onto the ceiling. (As a seasoned painter I hated stucco.) They said they were hired by the real-estate company to "spruce the place up a bit", but I was welcome to look around.

There was a large living-room with several small, cottage-type slider windows that offered no real view. Outside, blackfly city thronged. There was a room to the right, a stair case next to that, and a hallway adjoining, which led to a narrow back porch complete with the living tree branch.

Bonus. What it did have was hydro. I noticed a recently installed sixty amp fuse box next to a back door at the end of the narrow porch.

The rudest feature of the sprucing-up campaign was the entire downstairs wall surface, which had been covered floor to ceiling with the cheapest knotty pine paneling you can buy. It covered every room including the hallway and the upstairs. This stuff consisted more of mucilage than of wood. Punch a hole in it, and a chunk pops out the size of our fist. If you try to burn it, the smoke comes out green. This crap was the rage in 50's-style rec-rooms, but now it just doomed the place. I informed the workmen I might be interested, but only if they stopped their ruinous sprucing up.

On the second floor there was utter chaos. It looked like it had served as the fort for Spanky and Our Gang. There was no railing at the top of the stairs. There was nothing on the walls. The two rooms and a large room to the right of them were separated by two-by-four studs on sixteen inch centers. Yet the cathedral ceiling was supported by two massive pit-sawn timbers which I liked a lot.

There was no insulation in the ceiling, just plywood and asphalt shingles between me and the sky, which was something I didn't appreciate. Broken furniture and mattresses were scattered around. Decks of playing cards and poker chips littered the place, along with dozens of spent shot-gun cartridges. Arranged around the back window were some empty wooden crates. As I stood there taking in the mess, a large flock of ducks flew over the roof heading for the beaver pond. Probably they did so every evening about this time. Ah yes, this had been Canadian hunting at its best, playing cards, drinking beer, and shooting the occasional duck from a broken window.

Yippie yi yo kayah. Oink.

I stepped over to the window openings on the back wall. From this height the panorama was pure magic. The beaver meadow before me, the forest beyond, the chain of ponds to the right—it seemed timeless, peaceful, serene. There was a huge straggling oak tree in the beaver meadow, and as I watched the biggest blue heron I have ever seen glided out of the back ponds, caught the updraft from heat rising off the meadow, and seemed to float up into the oak tree, where it disappeared. I was pulled back to the exultant moment I had earlier experienced in the day when I stepped into the meadow.

If I knew then that it would take me ten years to turn this dump into a comfortable home, would I have been so eager to buy? If I had known that it would take me ten years to attain a measure of mindfulness, would I have chosen instead to remain an ignoramus? Renovations are wearisome, but realization takes everything you've got. The road ahead would be difficult. But then life is always difficult for someone who lacks discipline.

Joe Pye Weed

The die was cast. In pain English, a man's gotta do what a man's gotta do. I drove back to Minden, called the real-estate company, and made an offer. It said on title that the closing date was the end of November, 1988. It was now mid June, and I needed another $5,000 to close. I had lots of painting contracts, so I could paint like a madman for three months and move in by Christmas, hi ho!

I returned home and told my father I had bought a house at Halls Lake. He was less then ecstatic, but then my father was not the ecstatic type. All he said was how much he loved the sound of whippoorwills in the evening when he lay in bed at the cottage twenty-five years ago. His only comments concerning my behaviour, was to remind me that I was failure-prone.

Bless her heart, my sister, who also suffered MS with an onset ten years in advance of my own, was genuinely delighted. She loved Halls Lake and couldn't wait to come up and see the place and swim again at our beloved beach. She even went out and bought me a set of dishes.

Brenda, my beloved, was indifferent. On hearing my decision she said "Oh, that's nice." In any event I didn't see any of them for the next few months. I was painting seven days a week. Week ends, I could make $350 painting gone-with-the-wind staircases in pretentious new homes. I would actually move in temporarily, arriving Friday night with my equipment and a sleeping bag and leaving Sunday night with the job done. There are 350 rungs in a winding staircase, three coats of white paint, the railing once sanded, and three base coats of varnish twice sanded.

Whenever I got a break between jobs, I loaded the van with supplies and went to the Buckslide. The first time I brought Brenda, she looked around and immediately went to stay with a woman who lived nearby, a healer of German descent who advertised her services on a big highway sign under the name of **NO**. That was in mid-August.

After Brenda left, I went out to the well to bring in some pails of water. I had already cleared the brush and bushes from around the aperature. This was a ring-type well. It had a circular concrete lid, cut into the top of which was a chamfered concrete block designed to be lifted out. The concrete block itself was about fifty pounds in weight, not hard to raise in summer. The water level was about ten feet down. I had to learn how to throw a pail so it would sink and not just float around on the surface. Then, after it sunk, I pulled it up with a rope. Between pails I walked back to the beaver meadow. A flock of partridge flew up from behind the house, and there were song birds of every type singing from all different locations, and among them were ovenbirds that made a sound like a kid playing up and down on a mouth organ. The whole meadow was in seed. The colours had changed from the bright green of spring. Now yellow and sienna dominated with notes of blue from the chicory and masses of lavender from the Joe Pye weed, which grew up five feet tall, as high as the beaver grass.

Joe Pye was an Indian medicine man that used this plant to treat dementia. I am not sure what dementia is in technical terms, but I have a feeling that my whole distracted consciousness was one big mass of dementia, probably a by-product of MS. Maybe Joe was offering the path to mindfulness and clear perception. But the truth is, I didn't trust the aboriginals. It wasn't that I didn't like them. Rather, I avoided them because of what the great nations of Europe, of which I was a proud descendent, had done to them. I felt whenever I ran into them they had every right to split open my head with a tomahawk. My noble ancestors had taken to hunting them deliberately for sport, had given them blankets infected with smallpox, had abducted their children for purposes of molestation, had systematically erased their culture. It was all so horribly bad I couldn't deal with it mentally. When I met aboriginals I harboured a distrust of them, for surely, I reasoned, they must distrust me. But it also seemed that they could teach us how to live on the planet without destroying it. So there stands Joe Pye, lavender-lit among his namesake plants, offering assistance for my fractured mind.

Sorry Joe, sorry for you, sorry for me, and sorry for all of us.

I unloaded the van and tidied up as best I could. Brenda eventually returned and we spent the night listening to the beavers chorusing. I explained what I planned for the place, and she agreed to come up and spend Christmas with me there.

I had two months to get the place ready. I knew it would be cold, but I had no idea how cold this part of the world could get. Traveling between Oakville and Buckslide, I started calling the place home, because, like it or not, I now owned the joint and there was no going back. I haunted Salvation Army outlets, being big on quilts or anything else that was warm, serviceable and cheap. I already had a good selection of carpentry tools, and I bought a Franklin-style cast- iron woodstove, which was the going heating item back then.

Jumping the Snare

I moved up in November 1988, when the snow was already waist-deep. I had to push my supplies from the van over the snow into the house. Inside, it was bitter cold. I assembled the Franklin stove. To close off the upper floor, I put insulation on a sheet of plywood and manoeuvred it over the opening from the stairs below. I needed firewood, but first I had to shovel out a place to get the van off the road.

It was evening when I went to see Murray Walker to buy some firewood. Murray lived just two farmhouses off Walker's Line. Murray had ten brothers and sisters, and as I would soon learn, the road got its name from the fact that you could turn over a board anywhere on that road and find a Walker under it.

Sliding sideways into Murray's driveway, I quickly learned that my wallowing van was not the vehicle for this part of the world.

Murray's house and barn were in a state of advanced decrepitude. Lying about were farm equipment, horse drawn buggies, sleighs, wagons, one-horse ploughs, cultivators, windows, doors, wheels, pails, barrels. A few things new, most older than my own lifetime; some in use, most neglected by encroaching modernity; everything left mouldering from productive years gone by. I had travelled 200 miles north and 100 years backwards in time.

There was smoke coming from the chimney. I made my way to the front stairs and shouted "Hello this place!"

A loud voice hollered back "What the hell's going on there!"

An old fellow appeared, of indeterminate age, wearing a big black felt hat, rubber gum boots and many-layered clothing that looked as if he had just been mucking out the stables.

"Murray Walker's the name. Bark's worse than my bite. Come on in and I'll fix us a coffee."

I followed him through the porch, jumbled with chain saws, horse harnesses, ancient scales, bags of potatoes, seed, feed pails, and a dog of indeterminate breed. That dog was big. It might have been a German shepherd. Its fur was black and looked like the stuffing from an old couch.

"That's King," said Murray. "King's old enough to vote."

We went into the kitchen, which was like being transported back a century in time. Everything that had been brought into the kitchen and porch in the past however-many-decades ago sat right where it had been placed when last used. I sat down at the kitchen table while Murray made coffee. The kitchen table was so cluttered I couldn't see where he could put a cup. There was a large square woodstove throwing plenty of heat, but the window beside the table was missing completely. A huge work horse was looking in the window. Apparently Murray and the horse were good friends, but for those who weren't, he kept a .55 calibre Snider rifle nearby.

We talked awhile and I learned that Murray had lived here all his life. His mother had died eight years ago and he missed her every day. His ten brothers and sisters were all gone too. Murray was witty and downright funny, but hard as flint. He was happy in his place just the way it was. I should have learned something about simplicity right then, for I was a perfectionist, destined to spend twelve years building my place into something I thought someone else would like, a someone who never chanced to come my way.

After we had coffee we went out to his old farm truck and loaded it with dry firewood. It was getting dark when we got to my place. Murray of course knew the property, said it was the old Hown place, thought they abandoned it on account of the foundation problems. Great news!

We piled the wood right in the kitchen. Murray didn't think much of my stove. He said, "You won't get no heat out of that. You need a box stove." He left, saying he would stop in from time to time to see how I was doing.

Those first few years I still made occasional trips to Oakville to maintain friendships and pick up bulk supplies. By late 1991 I had 130,000 kilometres on my Toyota van, and as I had just made the last payment, if fate was kind I could expect to get at least 100,000 klicks more for free.

On a bright December morning I left Oakville with a load of ceramic tiles and a new table saw. I took the 401 to Highway 400 and turned north, skirting Toronto. The snow-belt that runs through Barrie was clear, but within a few kilometres the sky started getting real grumpy, a sign that a storm was blowing in from Georgian Bay. Sure enough, by the time I reached Gravenhurst a blizzard was pounding on the windshield as if it was sprayed from a fire hose. A little further on was the junction with Highway 118. It would be sixty kilometres to the stop-sign at Carnarvon, with hardly anything in between. For a long stretch there was not even hydro service. No poles, no wires, nobody.

The snow was coming down so heavy I had to put my head lights on low. On high beam I could only make out an impenetrable yellowish swirling wall. As the snow was piling up along the sides of the road, I had no choice but to drive straight down the centre. Suddenly a muscle truck, one of those tandem wheel jobs, tore past me in total silence, double my speed, kicking up huge plumes of snow. It forced me to swerve onto the right shoulder, and the van went into a sideways slide. As the show piled up against the wheels, I tried to correct, but the van flipped over onto its roof and slid down the embankment. Ploughing through the snow, it collided with a rock outcrop that split the roof and smashed the windshield. I was pressed forward into the dashboard. Everything in the back of the van tried to ram forward into the driver's compartment. I could see stuff shooting out through the windshield.

I came to a stop dangling upside down in my seat belt. The theme song from Shaft was playing on the radio. I hung there for awhile until I released the harness and fell onto the roof in a heap.

"Is anyone there?" a voice called out.

"I'm here!" I called back.

A bear of a man in coveralls pried open the passenger-side door and helped me out. "I'm so glad I came down to check," he said. "I told the missus I think there's steam coming out of that van. I better see if anyone's trapped inside."

This man probably saved my life with his keen observation and human concern, but in the excitement of the moment I never asked his name. The snow had almost stopped, and there was a gas station nearby. I reported the accident and phoned Murray Walker for a ride home. Murray hadn't ventured so far from the Buckslide since the days when he picked carrots down in Holland Marsh, so it took him a good ninety minutes at sixty clicks an hour to reach me. The van was a write-off. We loaded its contents into Murray's pickup and set out for the Buckslide. On the way home

Murray told a string of stories, most of them about the hardships of the past but always delivered with a humorous twist.

As Murray put it, "if the rabbit jumped the snare, we all ate potatoes"

Murray hadn't had a drink in ten years, but he told the story of the time he was put in jail for disorderly conduct. Well, he had a mickey of rum stashed in his boot, and half-way through the night the policeman said to Murray, "I think you're worse smashed now than when I locked you up," so he drove Murray back home and impounded his truck overnight.

Once I had my replacement vehicle – another Toyota, but this time a pickup with a long box – I would visit Oakville from time to time. But down there by the lake I never told stories about the likes of Murray Walker. Although he only lived two hundred miles away, Murray's reality was too far removed for my city friends to comprehend.

And now, come to think of it, so was mine.

Under the Quilts

I t took six months for my insurance claim to be settled, and in the meantime I had no vehicle. Except for the odd visitor who dropped by I had no means of getting down to town, so I was confined most of that winter to places which I could reach on foot. For someone living in the bush this can make for desolate times because the deep cold only intensifies your constant loneliness. Yet in tramping through the fields and woods I gained an appreciation for the delicacy of snow, which is never just plain white but can glow from mauve to rose with every colour and hue of the rainbow. I learned that the beaver meadow, even though it is shallow, was the last water to freeze up, probably because the decaying grasses released a certain amount of heat.

Anticipating a Christmas reunion with Brenda, I tidied up the place as best I could. I had brought drapes and such to make it look nice and cozy. I even had a phone installed. But Brenda didn't come, and that turned out to be the coldest, loneliest Christmas I ever spent. On Christmas Eve I went outside, which made me lonelier yet, because it was such a picture-perfect winter landscape. The canopy of stars was as if I could touch them. The pine trees surrounding the house were bent low with snow. The world was dead silent. Yet the beauty of it all only seemed to make my isolation worse, because I wanted so much to share these precious moments with someone I loved.

That winter, without the warmth of a companion, the only comfortable place in the house was to sit directly in front of the stove with my feet on the front fender—a stove which didn't hold enough wood, so it had to be loaded constantly. You could keep a drink at arm's length from the stove and it would stay icy cold. Just how cold did it get? Well, there's a rule-of- thumb, which says that for it to get cold enough to freeze a pail of water solid, it has to be twenty-five below zero inside the cabin. I would bring two pails of water from the well in the evening and set them in the entrance of my would-be kitchen. One night, while I was sleeping under my pile of quilts, both those galvanized pails froze so solid they spilt open along the seam.

Why, oh why, would Brenda want to stay down south?

Often when I pulled the pails up out of the well I would spill water around the square lid. One night I found the lid frozen in place from water spilt the night before. I tried to pry it loose with a large crowbar, but the lid, when it came free, went corner to corner, and when I tried to pry it out, it dropped right through, making a big, hollow-sounding splash. I had not thought to tie it off. This was an utter disaster. Somehow I would have to get the thing out.

With my brain addled with MS I completely panicked. As there was no-one to help, I decided I would have to go down into the well and fetch the lid myself. I thought about Murray and how tough he was. If I was going to live up here, I would have to become like him, and somehow I knew instinctively what he would do.

I reckoned the temperature was about twenty below freezing. It was eight feet down to the surface of the water in the well, and there was ten feet of water below that, to where the well lid was sitting on the bottom. I took an eight foot pry bar, what we used to call a "blue tip", and pried away the top ring of the well. This made a four foot diameter opening. I put my twenty-foot extension ladder down to the bottom. My biggest fear was that when I got down near the bottom the ladder would flop back to the inside of the well leaving me trapped beneath it. With no-one to talk me out of it, I put on a set of red flannel underwear, climbed down to the bottom of the well, felt around for the handle on the lid, fed a rope through it, and pulled it back up.

Isolated without a vehicle, that winter of 1992 was mostly just bone cold and lonely. In the course of my years on the Buckslide, the heating situation greatly improved, but I never was quite able to get over the loneliness. I had planned to take this step, and there was no way I was going to turn back now. But the execution of my new self-imposed life-style proved far more difficult mentally and physically than I could ever have imagined. In the winter I would put three or four vintage Salvation Army quilts on top of the bed to prevent the cold seeping up through the mattress from below. Then I would throw an equal number on top. Having thrown a new maple round on the woodstove, I would wait an hour or so until the area immediately around the stove and the kettle on top of it were warm enough to wash and prepare coffee. As it would be too cold to do anything practical in the house, I could only crawl back under my pile of quilts. Most of January and February I spent in hibernation, curled up shivering in the sack.

I experienced deep wells of depression as I lay huddled under those mangy quilts. Endlessly I would plan how I would turn this drafty dump into a dream home. In the beginning I hated the fact that I had tied myself to this place, yet I could see no other way but to go on in the direction I had chosen. Gradually as time went by I found a way of life I could abide.

During the time I spent under the quilts getting warm, I reflected on what I had until now perceived as being my biggest problems in life. One: I had no money. Two: I had MS. Yet weren't my issues basically the same for every person in life, namely, to find out how to be happy? If I could just be happy, the other two issues didn't matter. Besides, what if I spent all my time trying to make money and didn't succeed? Would I then never be happy? The same went for MS. What if being happy or having money was just the luck of the draw or a fate predetermined by my genes?

Curled up beneath the quilts, I reflected on my aunt Bess and uncle Percival. They were smart enough in their own way. To my eyes they seemed happy. But they had no money, which was strange considering their situation. Long before Tim Hortons and Dunkin' Donuts came along, uncle Percy had the idea of starting a donut shop. He looked around the city of Hamilton and recognized like those subsequent Starch Kings that there were a lot of office buildings to which he could cater, selling coffee and snacks at lunch breaks for steady money. Uncle Perse was twenty-five years ahead of his time in starting up the first donut shop on the corner of Canada and Locke Street, and those were the best donuts ever, made with the best ingredients ever, and anyone who tried one of uncle Perse's donuts would declare themselves ever afterwards a faithful customer. The whole family worked for the donut shop, but Uncle Dan drove the truck, so people called the place Dan's Donuts.

Prosperity was just around the corner. My mother took a business course in order to manage the books. She had said to uncle Perse, "Maybe I should do the books"; and he said, "Great, I haven't the time myself". Meanwhile uncle Mac was out back ditching a batch of donut batter that got away on him because he had added too much yeast. Then there was the time along the Jolly Cut when uncle Mac upended the three-wheeled pie wagon, though he couldn't even drive the two-wheeler. And Aunt Bessie, who also worked in the store, caught the help stealing quarters from the till but was afraid to say anything. And mom, now the book-keeper, found that Perse was losing twelve cents on every dozen donuts he sold.

End of party? Not quite yet. Perse figured that mom, who was not a Pinney by birth, was as wrong as she was young. To his mind, the real reason he was not making money was that he was not cranking out donuts fast enough. So he started a night shift, and that was what finally did him in. Perse went broke. But he felt so guilty, that instead of declaring bankruptcy, by golly Perse paid off that whole debt, helping keep the bank in the black each month for the next twenty years.

For all the upheavals, the heavy emotions, the heartache and sense of failure, one thing didn't change. Perse's family had no money at the beginning and they had no money at the end.

That I had no money and that I had MS were unavoidable facts. My task was not to let these conditions determine who I was. Much as I would like to change the location of the schoolhouse, it was here at the good old MS academy that I was learning the lesson of impermanence. Every time I thought I had found a way to live with my affliction, it changed for the worse, until finally I realized that nothing but nothing stays the same. In reality, things are neither better nor worse. They just are.

The Bear at the Fair

The sort of mad behaviour that I used to get the lid out of the well was typical of how I went about building my house. I had no-one with whom to discuss the order of work or the right way to do things, so I improvised. In any case I couldn't give up. I couldn't walk away.

That first winter was mostly spent trying to stay warm, while planning how I would build my dream home for next to no cash. My intention was to keep the style of a frontier Canadian farm house, because this would allow me to cannibalize abandoned dwellings in the vicinity, of which there was a fair supply. I would expect payment for the demolition work, but if that was not forthcoming, I would tear down a suitable structure for nothing. I once had been an antique dealer in Nova Scotia, at a time when there weren't enough antiques to go around. Scarcity encouraged me to make fake ones. I got so good at it that one of my creations was authenticated as being 150 years old. Some museum of canadiana snapped it up. If I ever visit that museum, I'll be able to prove I'm over 150 years and still counting!

But my all-time greatest fake was that house on the Buckslide. I built it to look 150 years old, a task that consumed twelve years. The kitchen I left for last, because I never believed I would live alone, and that when I found the woman I could share all this with, she should have the opportunity to choose how the kitchen would look. Over the next years my life narrowed in focus. While working on the house I became more and more in touch with nature. At the same time I drew further and further away from society, from the people and friends who peopled my urban existence. I worked endlessly on the house to justify my being there. Mostly I worked alone in ways that involved huge amounts of physical exertion, along with continuous pain and exhaustion.

I constructed a twelve-by-thirty foot deck on the back of the house overlooking the beaver meadow. This was where I spent my time when not working on the house. Gradually I became attuned to the sounds and subtleties of nature, the constantly changing interplay of colour, and the infinite shades of light and dark. I began to hear as never before. On the rare occasion when people would come to visit, which was usually in the spring and summer, I would invite them onto the porch after dinner to hear the wolf howl. "Oh," they would say, "I have always wanted to hear a wolf." So we would all flock out to the porch. But after five minutes of listening to the chorus of the meadow and watching the fireflies darting, everyone would resume talking, while I alone would continue harkening to the non-human sounds. People from the city have forgotten how to listen to anything but themselves. They tend to foist their own values and ideas on nature, as if nature existed for their benefit. In the whole meadow chorus each creature is separate onto itself, calling to its own species. When awareness identifies the howl of a wolf, even though it's no louder then the rest of the sounds, it pierces like a jagged crystal straight to your soul. In one instant it grabs your heart and wrenches you back to a primordial existence, holding you firm in its grasp.

I loved my family and I understood my friends, but year by year I found myself drawing away from them. Up on the Buckslide, as I gained his respect for what I was accomplishing, Murray Walker, that obnoxious reprobate, became my closest friend. A man from a bygone era, he grew up in a time when you had to be tough or die. Murray ploughed forty acres with a one-horse plough when he was thirteen. You didn't complain about black flies, you simply endured them. Murray didn't have running water, and by the end of the day working with a horse, he could get fairly ripe.

On their occasional visits to my place my folks would always look forward to hearing Murray tell his stories, because for all of his hardscrabble ways, Murray lost neither his sense of humour nor his love for the ladies. One hot summer day, to protect my family's tender sensibilities, I was inspired to set a fan on a chair by the window, to keep them upwind of my malodorous guest. But my sister, who was pretty perceptive, chided Murray anyway, suggesting that he might consider going for a swim sometime soon. Murray didn't miss a step. "Yep," he said "I was in last night and I found three sets of underwear I didn't know I had."

One time, while Murray was helping me haul some granite rocks from the truck into the house, I told him I was going to build a fireplace.

He asked, "So what are you going to put it on"

"On the ground," I replied. "It'll go from bedrock right through the centre of the house alongside the stairs."

"That's a good place for it, Pinney," was all Murray said.

Even when it came to such a major decision, Murray never questioned my judgment. Nor did he suggest that maybe I should be doing something else first, such as piping running water in from the well.

To lay a foundation for the fireplace, I had to get building materials around to the back of the house, where there was a window entrance leading to the basement. To convey water to the basement, I hooked together a series of eaves troughs to serve as a makeshift sluice. That contraption carried water raised from the well around the house, then down through the back window, where it emptied into an old milk pail which I found in the crawl-space under the house. I had already brought the sand, cement, wheelbarrow and cement hoe in through the same window. As there was only four feet of head room, being five-eleven, I had to work bent over. Once I started pouring I couldn't stop until the job was done. I poured three pails at a time into the eaves trough, then went down into the basement and mixed the cement. In this way I created a solid five foot cube, using 300 wheelbarrows full of concrete mix. The job almost killed me, and I was in bed for three weeks recovering from it while the concrete set. But at the end of it all I had the base for a rubble stone chimney.

Over the winter I studied how to build rubble stone fireplaces. The actual construction would take me another two years. When it was finally done, I calculate it weighed over forty tons. The fire heated the granite and the granite heated the house. It was permanent and rock solid. It was there on all fours like the bear at the fair.

Once, while resting between loads, I went to visit Murray. In front of his house he had rigged a strange contraption. It was obviously meant to be a turkey pen, but there were as many turkeys outside as in. While I was coming to terms with the thing, Murray came out with a pail of feed and warned me to keep the door closed, even though there were turkeys all over the yard and out on the road. As Murray fed the birds, I marvelled at the way he had constructed the pen, wiring together bedsprings, aluminum screen doors, snow fence, and other bric-a-brac.

I said, "That's quite a turkey pen, Murray."

Detecting a note of irony, he looked me in the eye and said, "I didn't use no level or no square."

We went inside for a coffee. Murray had just finished planting his corn, having waited as is the custom until hearing the first whippoorwill. Murray allowed that in spite of his fence, he had taken to staying up nights to guard the turkeys from the raccoons. As a joke I suggested that he shoot the coons for food.

"My brother Carl eats them," Murray replied. "Says they taste a whole lot like turkey and a whole lot like corn."

I built Murray a raccoon trap so he could get some sleep. He thought it was the greatest thing anyone had done on his behalf. He put the trap right by the front porch so he could show if off to anyone who came by. I told him to use bananas, which racoons love, for bait. I guess skunks do too, because Murray caught a skunk the first night he set the trap.

I learned as time went by not to go out of my way to help Murray, who was from another era with a different mindset. Best let him do what he was going to do.

Over a period of twelve years I gradually rebuilt the house. Upstairs, I finished four bedrooms with cathedral ceilings and lots of big windows. I spent a lot of time lying in bed at night suffering exhaustion either from tearing down other people's houses for scrap, or from building my own from scrap. But there was also the unrelenting exhaustion that is the hallmark of MS.

By the end of the decade I was confined to a manual wheelchair and a walker, though I could still manage to crawl up the stairs. Getting to the bedroom was a big effort, so I enjoyed my time in the sack all that much more. When lying in bed I could look up through the skylight and see the stars above me. The window beside me opened onto the beaver meadow, where I could hear the chorus of frogs, birds, and animal songs emanating from what amounted to a bird and wildlife sanctuary. In time I learned to identify certain individuals and their corresponding mates. I began to look forward to hearing from each of them. There were many species of frogs and toads, the latter of both tree and marsh varieties. One type of tree toad that started in late summer was particularly interesting because it sounded exactly as if the house was creaking. Since the original house was not built to any building codes, which I did nothing to change, for a long time those toads had me believing the place was crumbling around me.

With one screech the owl could silence the entire serenade.

The only welcome sentient being with whom I shared space was a very large un-neutered tabby tomcat. I called him George. One winter the day before Christmas the temperature dropped to 40 below and stayed there for a full month. On that first day George began showing up at my door. I could see he was totally wild and wary of me. Despite the cold, I left the door open for a few minutes and put a bowl of food down. I did the same the second day. On the third night he came in, as I was nowhere in sight. The fourth night he came in he stayed for twelve years. Right to the end he remained wild and wary of me. He would disappear for months at a time, only to stroll in the door as if he had been gone but a day. After several years living with George I came to believe he was the reincarnation of my father, who was also wild and wary of me.

Critters will be Critters

Once in my twenties I went deer hunting. The experience had a powerful effect on how I viewed other living beings. On that trip myelf and another fellow were keeping watch overlooking a field. I saw three deer break into the open area. They were out of range for me, but in easy range for my partner on watch. He, however, was a poor shot. After firing three shots, he only managed to scatter the deer in all directions. One of them ran into a marshy stretch of bush. I figured if I ran through the bush I could arrive at the far side just about the same time as the deer. Arriving there, I only had to wait several minutes until the deer broke cover about forty yards in front of me. It was an easy shot. Mortally wounded, the deer staggered straight towards me. It came within an arm's length. I looked directly into its eyes and I could see it was asking me for help. Then the being died.

This experience profoundly changed how I would relate to my fellow creatures, for it seemed to me that the deer was appealing to our shared nature as sentient beings. After that experience it began to dawn on me that we are not just related to each other as human beings, but that we are related to all living things.

I always prided myself as having a good relationship with animals. Now that I had so much time on my hands I craved some form of direct contact with other life-forms. I was never really cut out to live alone, and more than anything I craved female companionship. Yet I knew that on account of my physical condition any serious relationship would only lead to frustration and bitterness.

At various times of the year there were on my property almost every species found in northern Canada. I had already met most of them on, let's say, a casual basis, but now I had time to develop my communication skills. Besides, I was getting bored with the same old conversation while talking to myself. When relating with wild animals I had found most species were ready to be quite friendly as long as one stayed calm and didn't give signals of fear or undo excitement that would confuse them. I fancied I had also developed a sort of universal language that most animals found soothing, but which sparked curiosity. The rule is, most animals are hungry first and curious second. But admittedly, none of the above applied in the case of one old grizzly bear, which I encountered while prospecting for gold on the Goat River between Jasper and Prince George. In that case I resorted to that old stand-by—*RUN!*

Up on the Buckslide the only time I really felt threatened and in danger was when a group of raccoons took up residence in my own house. This situation developed because of my arrogant belief that I had a special gift for understanding and communicating with animals. In my area by late spring everyone would be complaining about the raccoons and how destructive they were. Murray was particularly incensed because he raised turkeys. Half the cost of raising turkeys was spent on feed, so if the raccoons ate the other half Murray would be wiped out. One day Murray came to my door in a black rage which had transported him beyond mere oaths and swear-words.

"Them damn raccoons ate ten of my fifty turkeys," he railed.

Frankly, it was hard to take Murray seriously at that point because of the outfit he was wearing. He had on his father's large black felt hat, which may have been fashionable back in the 1920's. He wore that hat at a rakish angle, revealing that it was much adorned with long white hairs from Fife, his cat, who slept on the brim whenever Murray put the hat aside. To complete the ensemble Murray wore several shirts, turquoise shorts with large greasy stains, and boxer underwear which, being longer than the turquoise shorts, struck two inches out the bottom like girlish frills.

Murray had good reason to be mad. He had been up all night, sitting on the porch guarding the turkey pen, which was only about fifty feet from the front porch. He wanted revenge and he had a plan. Someone—meaning himself— had hit a turkey with his car earlier in the day. Murray had tied the injured bird to his front porch with a piece of string. When night fell, he would wait on the porch with his shotgun cocked, so when the raccoons came to get the turkey it would be high gunplay at the Walker hacienda.

I said, "Sounds like a plan, Murray. Give em hell!" And with that Murray drove off.

Not more than fifteen minutes later his truck was back in my driveway and Murray was turning the air blue with some pretty bad language. He held up a string with a turkey leg tied to the end. Seems, that in the time it took Murray to drive over and reveal his Master Plan, a raccoon had stolen the turkey in full daylight, leaving just the one forlorn leg.

I advised Murray to get out of the turkey business.

But as I say, my own experience with raccoons was far more sinister, and it is one for which I must take full responsibility.

It started when I began feeding the raccoons around my house. My theory—which turned out to be a very bad theory—was that raccoons wouldn't rip up my garbage if I kept them well fed on kitchen scraps. I executed my plan by smearing peanut butter in the tree outside my front door. Peanut butter will infallibly attract a raccoon.

Sure enough, as the sun was going down I saw a large raccoon swinging from tree to tree to reach the one with the attractive smell. Two little ones followed. The next night I put peanut butter on the front door step, which was an even worse idea. Within a week, each night at precisely eight o'clock the raccoons would make a scuffling sound at the front door. I would open the door, greet the raccoons, who were now three in number, then let them into the kitchen. I put down three bowls of dog food, and they would eat one nugget at a time, looking up at me with their cute little faces. I would shake my head, meaning no more food for now, and they would all turn and file out the door.

It was all very sweet, but it was also very stupid. I would even have friends over in the evening to demonstrate our cosy domestic arrangement, explaining how clever I was in winning the raccoons over with just one bag of cheap dog food. Now that we had this loving bond, they would never again tamper with anything they shouldn't, including my garbage.

Of course, this was all egotistical nonsense, which kept me oblivious to the true nature of animals and their reality. Our four-footed friends don't possess egos or minds that are driven insane by a constant stream of thoughts about non-existent things. They live in the moment. They are not malicious by nature, but humans can cause grief by inflicting their own neuroses upon them. Animals spend their waking hours seeking food and protecting their shelter. I had corrupted their normal balance by providing an artificial food source, making them dependent upon me for their basic survival. Naturally, they would eventually begin to treat my home not only as a food source but also as their shelter. I was slow to recognize what was happening.

I also failed to realize that, far from being a large animal that could threaten smaller animals by swinging a big stick, I was now a slow-moving, laughable creature confined to a wheelchair. If I didn't understand the significance of this, the raccoons certainly did. They were taking my measure. Additionally, their number had grown to eight.

The front portion of the house consisted of a sitting room to the right, as well as the stone fire-place. A hallway led to a bathroom and to a laundry room hung with a solid pine door. At the end of the hall, sliding glass doors opened onto the back porch, where I spent most evenings watching the sun go down, believing myself in harmony with nature.

This was to be our field of battle.

One evening, as I sat in the gathering darkness I noticed a fat raccoon waddling along the window sill. He rounded the corner post and came onto the porch through an opening I previously hadn't noticed. He climbed up onto the overstuffed couch. I could just make out his outline but the bright yellow eyes were very distinctive. I was eating licorice allsorts at the time. I rolled over and offered him some. He reached out and took them one at a time, seeming to enjoy them. Then I noticed another raccoon approaching along the railing on the other side of the porch. He came over on the other side of my chair and also seemed to enjoy eating licorice. This became a regular occurrence. Whenever I spent evenings on the back porch, the raccoons would come just at dark and share whatever I had, be it popcorn, hotdogs, or their absolute favourite, bananas.

One day, having become engrossed in a good book, I abruptly terminated the routine. Instead of sitting on the porch, I remained in the library beside the fireplace. My custom was to hold a book with my right hand, while allowing my left to dangle down beside the wheelchair. The house was dead silent. Suddenly I was transported into heart-stopping, mind-numbing terror. From what seemed like the pits of hell a small monkey-like paw had reached up and grabbed my left hand. It felt leathery and horrible. In terror I looked down to see a large raccoon, which was checking as usual to see if I had treats for him. Finding nothing, he ambled off in the direction of the kitchen, stopping off to eat the cat food. I gave chase in my chair, and as I passed the hall I noticed the door at the end of the hall was firmly shut. So the raccoon had found another way in!

I chased it through the kitchen and out the front entrance to the living room and down the back the hall. As I passed the kitchen entrance for the second time I noticed another, even bigger raccoon dragging the whole bag of dog food out of the kitchen, intending to join up with the other in the back hall. They were definitely tag-teaming me. Raccoons laugh with a high, chucking sound which can be very chilling. That was the sound I heard as they took off into the night.

Right then, I knew I had a big problem. Several nights passed without incident; then on the third night, when reading the same book in the same place, I was startled by a loud crash. In a house as isolated as mine, a crash of this magnitude can be alarming indeed. I rolled to the entrance of the hall leading to the back porch. The door remained closed, but by now I had discovered that the raccoons had found a way into the bathroom by climbing up into the insulation above the back porch wall, and thence down through the closet. As I sat watching in astonishment, there was another, louder crash. This time I saw that the bottom of the bathroom door was bent in toward the hall about four inches. This door was a single slab pine door an inch thick. It was held shut by a wooden peg that turned on a screw. I could see that a couple more assaults on the door from the other side and the peg would go flying off.

After two more crashes, that is what happened. They were here. Three came into the hall, while one stayed back in the bathroom. I rolled towards them, hoping to drive them back into the bathroom, but this time they were giving no quarter. As I moved forwards they just spat and hissed at me, then scooted around my wheelchair into the kitchen to help themselves, paying no further attention to my presence in the house.

I went back to the library, where at least there was only one entrance, to consider my situation. First, I realized this was all my own doing due to my total lack of understanding of the beings around me. Secondly, I had unwittingly reduced my existence to the most primal and stupid expression of which humans are capable, namely *warfare*. I was in a battle to determine who would live in my own house. Would it be me or the raccoons? Since the problem was entirely of my own creation, I was not inclined to ask for outside help. While the raccoons trashed the kitchen, I plotted strategy. On their side was strength of numbers, but as to how many there were I couldn't be sure. Moreover, they clearly had superior powers of observation, excellent mobility in three dimensions, and a grasp on reality that was apparently keener than my own. On my side I had a .58 calibre Sharps cap-and-ball black powder rifle left over from my teens, when I was enthusiastic about long-distance shooting. That I would ever have to shoot another sentient being with such a weapon was to me unthinkable, at least until now.

The Sharps posed two problems. One, the only bullet mould I ever acquired for the gun was for pouring heavy buffalo slugs. The other problem was that the weapon took 120 grains of black powder. If I discharged it inside (like those duck hunters of yore) it would instantly fill the house with thick choking black smoke. The first problem would do serious damage to the trim work; the second would ruin the air quality while blotting out visibility. I had kept a quantity of both poured bullets and black powder from times past. The bullets were obviously still good, but about the powder I couldn't be sure.

In arranging for my defence, I made a cylindrical paper cartridge using a piece of dowel. Into this I slid the buffalo slug. Next, after gluing it along the seam, I filled the cartridge with black powder and twisted off the far end. Then I placed the paper cartridge into the breach. The block cut the extra paper off when I closed the breach and put a primer cap in place. Now I was ready to shoot a buffalo. True, I had a bit too much gun for raccoons. But I was not going to abandon my house to a bunch of varmints on that account.

I decided the only way to preserve the house was to open the porch sliding doors, lie upon the living room floor, and shoot down the hall towards the back porch, in the direction they would come. I had chosen a paper cartridge as opposed to pouring the powder directly into the breach because the additional burning paper would give a more impressive muzzle blast.

Jesse the Shooter lay under an old carpet, with the Sharps pointed down the hall. About 8 o'clock there was movement at the end of the hall. First one racoon came in, then two more behind it. The hall was quite narrow so it wasn't too hard to line them all up. The discharge of the Sharps was like a thunderclap. The flame from the muzzle extended the length of the hall. When the smoke finally cleared, the racoons and the screen at the back of the porch were gone. There was a racoon on the back porch that appeared shell-shocked. I pushed him out the door and watched as he staggered away.

From that day forward ole Jesse would strive to be more mindful as to how his actions, if directed by selfish concerns, could end in the destruction of that which he loved.

I couldn't take a lot of time to dwell upon the incident. I just learned from it and moved on. You can't be an armchair philosopher if you depend upon a disability pension as your primary income. There was just enough government money either to remunerate my parents for looking after me (perish the thought!), or to pay for a nursing home. It was hard to hold down a mortgage and build a house at the same time, but I simply learned to make do. My primary concern was to get the heavy work done before the MS rendered me wholly incapable.

The Calling of the Loon

I was a worrywart by nature, but finally I managed to pay off the mortgage. That was the day I had foreseen so long ago, the day I had envisioned with Brenda and myself as proud owners. Once the bank was off my back I had planned to buy a place down south to avoid the winter cold, which is particularly severe for someone with MS. However, the forty acres that surrounded my one-acre came up for sale just then. The man who lived across the road was a kill freak and a bully, and he had told everyone that he was going to buy the land at the first opportunity. He even told me he intended to put a duck blind on the beaver dam behind my house. Another neighbour, who was an environmentalist and a good friend, owned the land on the other side of the beaver dam. He had helped me put up simulated houses to bring wood-ducks back to the area. He was all too familiar with the individual who intended to buy the land, and so he offered to help with the down payment if I would intervene in the sale.

That was how I came to own forty acres, instead of a beach-house in Costa Rica. To stay warm I now had the back forty to cut for fire wood. But now I was also responsible in some sense for every living thing on those forty acres, some of which, like the old growth white pine, had been there for hundreds of years. The reason I enjoyed such a diversity of wildlife stemmed from the fact that the forty acres formed a complete watershed, with the beaver dams draining into Halls Lake. Most species need such an environment; otherwise, if it is disrupted, they disappear.

Here I was, king of all that I could survey. From this perspective I could see how the planet was being rendered uninhabitable through the institution of private ownership. In my case I looked after everyone as a good steward should. But years later, when I had to take refuge in a nursing home, my land was sold to pay for my upkeep. Over time I learned to survive the nursing home, but the wildlife was not so lucky. The subsequent owner trashed everything within a year of my departure.

Hey, Joe Pye, can two-footeds, selfish and short-lived, actually own the land?

At Halls Lake I built a good, solid, liveable house. That was a practical accomplishment in which I take justifiable pride. From being nothing but a fake English Painter, I eventually became a competent, if eccentric carpenter. But it was my inner maturation that counted most. These years spent in the bush taught me that all the worry, fear, anger and depression that had dogged me my whole life were an utter waste of time and energy. These were states of mind which

I myself created and sustained. I alone was responsible for all that misery. I had turned away from the bliss which is everyone's birthright. To enjoy life is really all we need to do for the whole stretch, from the cradle to the grave. The rest, as they say, is just a haircut and a shave.

From delving into various spiritual traditions I understood mentally that existence is impermanent. But how could I make this perception work for myself, as someone riddled with the stealthy creep of multiple sclerosis? MS undercut every adjustment I made to reality. No sooner did I achieve a level of comfort, than it would knock out another rung. I wanted impermanence to slow down at the very least from a gallop to a trot. Yet my deteriorating condition hardly gave me time to adjust to the previous state, before I was confronted with another concession that restricted my mobility, messed with my mind, and shrank my horizons.

Eventually the day came when I realized that if I didn't stop driving I might start killing people instead of just raccoons. I had been using a walker, plus anything I could reach for support, to access my old Pontiac Catalina 2-Door. It was the only car I could get into and out of under my own steam, because the door was nearly as big as an entire compact car. One day, approaching the brand-new stop-light in Carnarvon, I found that I couldn't lift my foot from the floor to the brake pedal. There was a split second of panic until I registered no cars at the intersection and sailed right through unscathed. But I realized afterwards that I had just driven what amounted to a small tank way too fast through a red light. With the racoon fiasco fresh on my mind, I resolved then and there to quit driving. This decision dramatically shrank my area of activity to the inside of the house and the immediate environs. Now I couldn't shop for groceries or interact with other people unless they came to visit me.

At various points in my life I had puttered about as an artist, but though I showed talent, I never had the discipline or the focussed concentration to excel. Now that I was virtually immobilized, I had plenty of time on my hands to determine if I was good enough to satisfy myself as the first and foremost critic. My notion of what was "good" was still cock-eyed, but by undertaking this work I learned a profound lesson: When you are totally focussed, your disability no longer matters. The trick is to embark on a project that takes one hundred percent of your concentration, leaving no room for the endless dialogue that plagues most humans who suffer pain. Such deep absorption can take care of the daylight hours, leaving only the nightmares to deal with in bed.

The fact that I craved approval was one affliction that I couldn't blame on MS. Another problem was that I couldn't grant due recognition to my own work. Perhaps both of these human failings led me to strive for the highest quality production, which finally weathered my fiercest self-criticism and thus freed me in the end. In taking up first the carving knife, then the brush, I connected with my father, who taught me at an early age to become one with what I wanted to draw. I, who had talked so much about my concern for animals, would now have to become one with them.

Carving loons is a common hobby here in cottage country. Often enough I had criticized the carvings I had seen at shows and fairs, commenting snidely that the carver had fashioned nothing but a plain old duck, painted over to look like a loon. Wanting to demonstrate that a loon was in no way just a gussied-up duck, I chose to carve the perfect loon for my first art project. From the fact that the frogs, as good loon food, were disappearing in the beaver meadow, I knew that future generations would not appreciate how beautiful a loon was. I felt an obscure obligation to the loons and to the future witnesses of the objects I was to create.

At night-time I had heard loons calling from the beaver dam, while I worked and schemed. It was as if their weird, sad song evoked the suffering of all living beings, fearful of the future and of the past. Through observation I learned what loons did and how they did it. I realized that loons, facing extinction, were the sleek dinosaurs of our time, and I wondered if the dinosaurs in ancient times also made beautiful sounds.

In this devotion I was a perfectionist. I carved two loons exactly as loons are. It took me two years working every day to complete them, and I am satisfied that I left an exact record of how they appeared. First, I carved the head and body without the feathers. Then I shaped each feather out of veneer and glued all ten gazillion of them to the body until they were perfect in their resemblance.

From there I went on to carve all the birds I saw around me, a task that took several more years. As with the loons,

I learned everything I could about each bird and why their feathers were shaped the way they were. This intense, shamanistic focus kept me distracted from the relentless progress of my illness. While in bird trance I existed outside the illness zone. When loneliness and isolation threatened to drag me down, I kept focussed on my art. In the midst of this work, I felt I might be going crazy with obsession, so I discouraged people from coming to visit, even though I yearned for companionship.

In striving for such perfection there was still a very human element, for I continued to seek recognition and acclaim for my art. After the spate of birds, I carved a twenty-foot totem pole with a huge eagle on top that looked as if could actually fly. That pole was put on display in Carnarvon, but only a few years later it broke into pieces while being reburbished. The last bird I completed was a six-foot blue heron. In gluing the very last feather to the wing tip, I stood up from the wheelchair unassisted for the last time.

Out of pain and suffering came beauty, but I was indifferent to money. Pieces of work on which I laboured thousands of hours, sometimes over years, I gave away or exchanged for groceries. The loons went to Australia after my antipodal cousin came to visit. Where once there were no loons in Australia, now there are two, though breeding is out of the question.

As the MS took more and more away, I chose to focus on the infinite grace of living things. When I could no longer manage to gather the materials to carve and sculpt, I went back to oil painting. In those last days, when I could still get around with a walker and canes, I suffered a lot of falls. While recovering, I studied light and shadow, the physical pain focussing my mind into pinpoint accuracy. The act of painting was pure survival for me. When I wasn't at the easel, I could at any moment tumble into a grey morass of formless depression without time or light, a limbo world that offered nothing to hold onto, nothing to pull myself out, and no direction to go, even if I was able.

Still I perceived myself as a separate being, a sharp-shooter separate from all except the quarry. I created beauty, but in my increasing abjectness I also drove beauty away. I could never actually embrace the object of my devotion. While painting I was focused purely in the moment, but as soon as I put the brush down I fell backwards into the past, mourning the man I once was and all that I once had aspired to be. Though I knew it as spiritual admonition, in my depths I did not realize that the past is an ever-changing fable woven by my own mind. It is a dangerous adversary indeed, one who constantly threatens to overwhelm an unconditioned sense of the present, one who cannot be defeated with counter-memories, one who refuses to negotiate and never sleeps. That exactly defines my thinking mind, which acts as if the past constitutes the present.

I couldn't blame my wretched state solely on the MS because my sister is likewise afflicted, yet she has a completely different approach to managing her life. Unlike me, Julie isn't one to isolate herself from society and friends. A year before being diagnosed she had given birth to a son. Her condition thirty years later, if anything, was more advanced than mine. Yet because she had raised her son and given him the compassion and understanding it took to guide him while her illness progressed, she had gained a wealth of knowledge which she could then draw upon to guide her brother—myself—through this seemingly endless quagmire. During those long winter months when I was confined to the house, I didn't need my sister's advice to realize that my decision to live alone in isolation was turning out bad. I longed for human companionship, but on those rare occasions when I reached out to my mother or sister, I really had nothing to say, because one day led to the other without much variation.

The Tethered Heron

Being mortgage-free and with the help of a good neighbour I was able to purchase the forty acres around my property, including the narrow strip between the back beaver dam, about five hundred yards from my house. As the new proud owner, this intriguing niche would be my first destination on the grand tour.

Some years ago I had owned a Yamaha 500 All Terrain Vehicle with foot controls, which was to serve me on local jaunts after I gave up driving. I built a ramp along the side of the house so I could drive the ATV flush with the back porch. There I would dismount and employ my walker in its stead. When I could no longer raise my foot, I sold that ATV.

One January, after being isolated in the house for five months, I responded to an advertisement for a brand-new, hand-operated Honda ATV. No money down, just come on down and sign on the dotted line. Though I could barely drag myself around with an aluminum walker, I reasoned to myself that this would be a sensible purchase. The hand controls got around my paralysis problem, and if I ever got stuck, I could extricate myself with the 2,000 lb. Stuart Warn Winch that came with the machine. In my current state of mind this meant I couldn't get stuck, period. At some level I knew that my reasoning was wrong, but the problem with slow progressive MS was that I constantly imagined doing things from the perspective of a former capability, not according to what I was able to do now.

I spent January till May in confinement with that new Honda sitting in a lean-to beside the house. The first warm day in mid-May and I was raring to go. I was dressed in running shoes, khaki pants, and a heavy plaid shirt, but no helmet. I dragged myself outside on my walker and saw on this beautiful sunny morning that there was still snow lying here and there in patches.

I got alongside the ATV with my walker. Holding myself erect with my left hand on the walker and my right on the seat of the ATV, I lay face down across the seat, and with a rope loop tied to the far foot rest, I pulled my body till I was mid-point across the seat. Next, reaching the handle grip with my right hand I swung my body around, still face down, until I could straddle the seat. Now facing forward, I was ready to go.

I told no-one that I was heading out through the bush. For somebody in my condition that was plainly insane, but an inmate who's just escaped prison doesn't go around blabbing about liberation either. I felt exhilarated just being outside, and now I was suddenly in a transfigured world as I started down the road with the warm sun on my back. I could smell the green freshness of spring.

I drove along the Buckslide till I reached the township road which bordered the one side of my property. The land which I had just purchased was covered in deep bush, thick, dark and mysterious. A ravine ran alongside the road with a small creek at the bottom. This creek flowed into the open beaver meadow, which was still flooded at this time of the year. The beaver grass had not started to show through the water, though by mid-summer the whole meadow would be dry and the Joe Pye weed would be waving five feet high.

Since I couldn't cross the flooded meadow, I tried to drive around the end on the high ground, where I thought it would join with a narrow strip of cedar trees between the front and back beaver dams. I was relying on a mental map that was void of detail, but this was of little concern to a fellow addled by Ms and half-crazed with cabin fever. Besides, if I should ever find myself in trouble, I had that Stuart Warn 2,000 lb. winch to get me out. As I drove into the deep bush, the temperature dropped from sunny and warm to damp and chilly. I found an old wagon path from years ago, which with its muddy sinkholes would nowadays take nothing less then an ATV to traverse. Undaunted, I pressed on until reaching higher ground. By then I realized that I had to stay with the bike wherever it took me—and that was hopefully back home. Further down the trail I entered a canopy at the highest part of the property, where there had been a homestead many generations ago. There was no evidence of the former dwelling, just a cleared acre surrounded by old-growth forest and some ancient apple trees. This was all that remained as evidence that a family once lived here, protected on three sides by water, totally isolated in a self-sufficient little paradise.

Had they been draft dodgers from the War of 1812? Whatever the reason, these were folks who didn't want to be found. As I imagined their home, and pieced together how they lived, I had the sense that there was no real difference between myself and them, that past and present were the same, and that if I were to move my house here, my act would be just a continuation of what had gone before. I didn't feel I owned this land, but was part of it. The field was growing back in, and the human family was no more, but otherwise what had changed?

I drove to the end of the field, where I thought the house would have been. From here the land went back into bush, declining abruptly towards the row of cedar trees between the front and back dams. I started down the slope. Before I had gone very far I realized that I had gone around too many trees to back up, but that it was also becoming too steep to go ahead. The only viable route was to the right, which would take me to the edge of the beaver meadow across from my house. Through the trees I could see that once I reached the water's edge, then maybe l could skirt the pond. The descent was very steep, but I made my way down to the water, where it was bright and sunny, and that soon made me feel better. I could see the back of my house about five hundred yards across the open water, the new year's growth of beaver grass not yet having obscured the view.

There were a few odd snags still standing, but most were lying on the surface or just under the water. I couldn't drive to the right as there was a large fallen tree blocking the route. This meant I had to go left, but only if the years of accumulated beaver grass managed to support the ATV. I only just ventured out from the shore when the bike sunk to its axles yet nevertheless held firm. The water was cold but bearable, and I was actually going in the direction I had planned, towards the back beaver dam, where I had seen a huge blue heron fly out every summer morning for almost twenty years.

I knew from my neighbour, Mary Oliver, who was 104 years old when she died, that that same blue heron (or one very much like it) had been nesting around the back Beaver dams for 150 years. Mary's father also remembered it from the time when those beaver dams had been completely isolated from the rest of the world. Perhaps that forgotten family on the one-acre of land had watched the big heron, too.

I was ruminating in a state of reverie on such matters when I struck something hard and got stuck. I tried to back up, but being in water up to the axle on wet beaver grass provided no traction. This didn't worry me too much, since I had that 2,000 lb. Stuart Warn Winch in reserve, but it did mean

I would have to get wet. I took plenty of time to view my situation. I had just rounded a corner, so I couldn't see my house anymore, but behind me there was a stump sticking above the water onto which I could hook the winch cable. The controls for the winch were on the handle bars. I would have to release the winch cable, then get into the water. It was numbing cold. With just my head above water I pulled myself along with submerged strands of the beaver grass. I wrapped the cable around the stump, then used it to pull myself back to the ATV.

I had to mount the bike in the way I had when I started out, except that by now I was very cold. I started the winch. As the slack tightened up, the the ATV tipped sideways, but did not move backwards even one inch. The next time I applied power, the stump came clean away and started nosing towards me. Now this was definitely bad, much worse than immersing myself in the frigid well next to the house. I would have to get back into the water, pull myself over to the stump, unfasten the cable, then carry it across the deep water to the shore line on my right, where there were some solid trees that I could use as anchors.

After much effort I managed to fasten the cable to a tree on shore, only to experience the same damn outcome as before. The sudden loss of faith in my trusty winch was attended by the gradual realisation that I was in very deep trouble. An underwater stump was jammed firmly between the engine and the frame of the ATV. Nothing I could do was going to make that vehicle move. l was trapped. This was not the first time I had been in a tight spot, but considering my options it could well be the last. The fact was I only had one option left, and that was to crawl home.

Hand over hand, I used the cable to make my way to shore. The bushes and brambles grew right to the edge and the mud was so slippery that I had to struggle for traction. Despite these obstacles, I made it to the first deadfall pine. Had I been wearing my helmet, I might have crashed through the branches head-first. As it was, the effort to push through was painful and time-consuming. A second spiny deadfall waited for me on the other side. This time I attempted to boost myself over the top, only to get hung up in the branches. For a brief time I hung in mid-air like a pig on a spit, only to crash down amid the brambles on the other side.

As I lay there catching my breath, I realized that I could no longer crawl. My boxer shorts underwear had slipped down to my knees, while my khaki pants remained tight on my hips. To free my knees, I would have to break the button at the top of my fly in order retrieve my underwear. I rolled around and tugged and cursed to no avail. Congratulations, you Chinese workers, who do such a good job sewing on buttons while supporting a family of ten on three cents an hour!

I was now reduced to crawling on my elbows like a conscript under fire. I made for the edge of the beaver dam directly across from my house, sometimes rolling sideways until I ran into a tree or became entangled in bramble. My sleeves were torn off and my elbows were bloody by the time I broke clear of the brush.

Resting waist-deep in water with my back against the bank, I saw that it was still a glorious sunny day. The sun was warm on my face, and there across the beaver dam was my house, looking just great with its different shades of yellow and brown steel roofing. Though chosen more for economic than aesthetic reasons, the effect was pleasing to the eye and harmonized well with the environment. Taking pleasure in the moment, I also realized that being so far from the road, no-one would see or hear me, and that therefore I was going to die.

That I was about to die didn't bother me very much. Going by the sun I judged the time to be about two o'clock, and I reflected on how accurately I could tell time, and that in an era when so many people had personal computers, I still hadn't owned my first watch, which was not quite true, because when I lived in Nova Scotia and had my antique business, to keep in character I wore a vest with a key-wind Moon railroad watch. Attached to that watch was a sling of chain which ran to a tiny pistol tucked in the fob; and that pistol probably worked better than the watch, but for that you needed a supply of old phonograph needles and primer caps, plus a penchant for playing high-stakes poker. I presumed my antique watch told railroad time in the years before Sir Sanford Fleming invented time zones, an innovation pretty much overlooked by a public enthralled by perforated postage stamps. All aboard for Yoyoville...

My god, why was my mind rambling now, of all times? If I couldn't stay in the moment under these desperate circumstances, surely enlightenment would be many life-times away. A scream from a circling raven snapped me back. Was that a Buddha-bird or a starving raptor?

I was very cold. The sun was still warm, but the water in which I was sitting was frigid. At night the temperature would drop about twenty degree, and I had no way to defend myself from whatever critters might come to feast on my hide. My first order of business was to free my legs, which were still bound at the knees by my fallen undershorts. Across the beaver dam, about fifty yards away, I spied a half-submerged deadfall. I could make out the stub of a limb. I guessed most of the deadfall in this meadow was black beech, good and strong. To solve my first problem, I would have to get to that log.

Aligning myself parallel to the water-edge, I pushed off from shore face down, propelling myself by clutching at tufts of beaver grass. My breath became ragged and my ability to inhale was impaired by the cold. Bumping up against the deadfall, I located the branch stub. My hands were so numb that I had difficulty getting my zipper down. I manoeuvred myself over the limb till it was sticking up through my fly. Then I bunched my knees up against the log and pushed off with all the strength I could muster. At last the button broke. Now I could reach my undershorts and free my legs. Putting a stick between my teeth to stop them chattering, I crawled along until I could see George, the cat, sitting on the back steps, watching my antics.

The story is told about a disciple of Buddha who was supremely blessed with the company of three enlightened beings, all of them cats. In his enlightened way George disappeared when he recognized I wouldn't need his assistance in transmigrating to the next world. Not this time, anyway. Shaking uncontrollably from hypothermia, I dragged myself up the back steps. Lying on the porch, I could not believe I was back home, safe. The bright red ATV was just a tiny speck in the distance. Everything around me was unreal.

Was I here on earth for some reason? Did I have some mission yet to accomplish? With every passing day, as my functions deteriorated, that noble prospect seemed less and less likely. But now, after today's experience, there was one thing I knew for sure: No longer could I trust the judgment of a mad man—myself—to steer a sane course through life. Blindly, insanely, I had put myself at mortal risk. Now I would have to leave this house by the beaver meadow and rejoin the human world, not as a master of the art of multiple sclerosis, but as a humble critter needing help.

Falling through the Cracks

Well, I've lost my equilibrium
And my car keys and my pride
The tattoo parlor's warm
And so I hustle there inside

Tom Waits, "The One That Got Away"

While living on the Buckslide those many years I never once used prescription drugs. When back pain or leg spasms kept me awake at night I would smoke pot for relief. What other medicine makes healing such a refined pleasure?

Up on the Buckslide I performed self-catheterization. Because I was careful with the procedure I developed a bladder infection only once every three years or so, which was remarkable in its way. But when an infection did take hold, it combined with the MS to make me extremely weak, as if I was coming down with the flu. Feeling like this one day in the spring of 2003, I crawled upstairs to my bedroom and opened the window so I could listen to the beaver meadow. I slept—or rather passed out—until the next day. I woke to find I couldn't move. I was still sure I only had the flu, but that for some odd reason my limbs were incapacitated. Then I heard someone enter the front door and a voice called out "Hey, mon, you alive or dead, mon?" It was Kevin, a buddy who lived on the next big lake to the south.

I managed to call out, and Kevin came up to my bedroom. I told him that I had the kind of flu that left you paralysed. Kevin said that I didn't look good and that I should go to the hospital. With that he took me by the feet and dragged me down the stairs. It turned out that I had sepsis resulting from a long-term bladder infection which I didn't detect because I had no feeling there.

I know it's a bad joke when you're talking about catheters, but this was the final straw. With a whirl of decisions and a lump of regret I sold my Buckslide property and bought a house in Minden that faced on the Gull River. In back there was a garden and a spacious shed that was serviced with hydro and a water hook-up, and there I cultivated sclerosis-specific cannabis. The house itself had a big kitchen so that I could manoeuvre around in my wheelchair, and there were sliding glass doors that gave me easy access to the back porch and to the garden beyond via a ramp. With my motorized chair I could wheel past the beer store, the liquor store and the TD bank, enjoying the human throng in the mode of Minden's very own Stephen Hawking.

To make ends meet I took in tenants. Since they had to pass through my living room to get upstairs, there always seemed to be somebody around to relieve the loneliness. I missed the serenity of the beaver meadow, but basically it was good now to have people around.

The crisis hit in December of 2008. A freak storm dropped 147 centimetres of snow on Minden in eight hours. They called it a "meteorological anomaly", except it was on the order of the white squall which C.B. Sheldon had the misfortune to sail into aboard his ship; or maybe it was more like the photosynclastic-infundabulam that Kilgore Trout encountered aboard his space craft. No doubt this storm rivalled the one in which I totalled my van seventeen years before. It was incredible to experience at the time, but like that earlier storm it came with a bad hangover.

Sitting on the back porch, I could actually hear the snow falling. Just the sheer weight of it coming in contact with the ground sounded like a far-off fog horn. The back porch lights turned the blizzard into a yellowish-white, frilly curtain. Beyond that I could see no further than ten feet. Katie, the upstairs tenant, and her four-year-old son came down to join me. Katie tried in vain to shovel the back porch and the wheelchair ramp to gain access to her car. Meanwhile, Ozzie, her son, was having quite a ball. He would wriggle into the newly created snow banks, and then Katie would reach in wherever she saw movement and pull out an animated little snowman waving his stubby arms and legs.

That night the storm prevented my personal support workers from coming to assist me into bed, so I had the rare pleasure of staying up late. When bedtime finally came I found it was no big deal to use a transfer board to ease myself over from the power chair. But the reverse was not so easy. After numerous futile attempts I fell back and waited for help. Due to the storm, help did not come for three whole days.

Anticipating more bad weather, my advocates urged me to take refuge in a nursing home for the winter. I signed a document and two days later I was deposited in a ward that catered to incapacitated stroke victims. There I stayed until springtime, holding onto my sanity by a thin thread. Later, as my physical condition worsened, I was forced to sell my Minden property and take up residence in the local long-term care facility. With much help from my friends I moved there on December 18, 2009. This is where I am today. I share a common bathroom with a person who borders on the vegetable state. When he dies, some other zucchini will take his place.

Up on the Buckslide I learned to go happily for days without seeing another human being. Yet I have never felt so alone and isolated as in this nursing home, where very old people, many suffering from dementia, shuffle around or doze away their final hours. I turn away from these ghosts to spend quality time with my computer, which has a special keyboard and a small flat-screen. Laboriously I transcribe my stories, then have my friends fix the spelling and sort out some jumbles, for I no longer have the use of my hands to paint or carve or even hit the right letter. It is really galling for a old marksman to miss such an easy target.

My computer keeps me in touch with the world beyond Minden, supplying me with Netscape movie downloads and with current news from various alternative websites. I don't think it is due merely to my decrepit state that I sense catastrophe brewing. Pug ugly beings have barged their way to the top of the heap. Even on my little flat screen their hypocritical smiles cannot disguise how much they hate life. These imps have formed a gang called the IMF, which is meant to spread sociopathy into the far corners of the world. Maybe they are not to blame for their rogue behaviour on the grounds that they have been hypotized by giant space lizards; but regardless, I would like to see our fearless leaders immobilized with multiple sclerosis before they carry us right over the cliff.

I began studying Zen around the time when I could no longer contribute to the world through my paintings and carvings. In the course of my reading I was drawn to the work of Pema Chodron, the good-hearted abbess of a retreat centre on Cape Breton Island. Pretty soon, though, I also came across the big money grab. Someone convinced me to pay $65 to participate in a virtual retreat beamed from an amphitheatre in California. I sat in my wheelchair staring at the screen, watching a crowd of silent meditators struggle with their impulse to yawn, stretch, or scratch their ass. For me, with sclerosis creeping into my fingertips, there wasn't much to learn there.

Though I obviously don't sit in a Buddha posture, I still meditate in the morning and at night, focusing chiefly on my breath. It's a moot question whether my MS imposes special obstacles that normal people don't encounter, because for one thing I don't know any other state of existence; and for another, I no longer try to picture what normal means. It was my lot in life to be stricken with MS, but maybe others are working off heavy karma in less physical ways on the mental and emotional planes.

The only place where peace and happiness can dwell is in this present moment. For me, the best way to be in the moment, where all sentient beings have the innate right to reside, is by smoking a pinch of vegetable matter that causes no measurable harm. Pot brings me physical relief while keeping suicidal thoughts at bay, and in the two years I have lived in this House of the Dead, not one day has passed when I have not gone outside to smoke a joint. Sometimes I would linger in the designated smoking zone, where I could get a resident to light me up. Besides, from my own experience with MS, I figured that people suffering from the ailments of old age could use a puff themselves now and then.

But there were occasions when some inmate complained that I was contaminating the air. Presumably a person like that would be very comfortable living in one of those dank apartment blocks where toothless pensioners drink cheap whiskey and chain-smoke cigarettes.

"How about you let me get high," I told them, "and I'll let you commit suicide."

In this ghost world I forgot how vindictive people can be; nor could I imagine someone actually finding the gumption to inform on me. But twice the nursing staff invaded my private space, rummaged through my belongings, grabbed my smoking kit, and called the cops. Both times I was charged with possession, though the charges were later dropped.

It turns out the Minden jail cells are not wheelchair accessible.

Too bad for the bureaucrats that my friends in the community held a benefit concert on my behalf at the Dominion Hotel, which is only a few minutes from the nursing home if you take the trail through the grove above the Co-op. The feature attraction was a kick-ass local band called "Bucket of Shrimp Ears". During the speechifying part of the evening somebody presented me with the Golden Spliff award (which was actually a yellow banana), and for all my woes I collected no less than $600 in donations that night. But please don't tell the tax man about that!

Too bad for Big Nurse, now that I have my medical marijuana permit. She will have to sniff around in someone else's drawers.

And too bad for me that no-one designed an electric rolling machine for us MS potheads who no longer enjoy the use of their fingers. As there's no-one on staff whom I trust to roll a decent spliff, that means I have to leave my stash off-site with a buddy in town. He's got steady hands alright, but he's wasting away with cancer, so sooner or later I shall have to find another recruit. Yet even with his help I still have to contrive a way to light the thing, and these days with my fingers gone rigid and twisted I find that Seafarer safety wood matches provide the only good scratch.

One solution to my predicament, known as a Vaporizer, I just heard about a few months ago. The vaporizer heats the cannabis inside a metal tube just to the temperature at which the psychoactive components gassify, leaving the harsh factors unburnt. I would have to test one for the high, but packing a tube is way less bothersome than rolling a joint, and from a legal angle the technology is quite appealing. Since in the strict sense of the term I would not be lighting anything, I would not be violating the establishment's smoke-free regulations. For someone in my situation, who had a lit match get away from him and ignite a paper grocery bag, a grey area like this is worth exploring.

Another day passes. I look out the narrow window at the drab landscape. An early thaw has left blotches of mud amidst the snow drifts. The hill is where it always is. The sky moves on. I have no real hope of leaving this place, where my fingernails grow as the hours pass.

There is still no cure in sight.

Even if this body withers away, I would like to stay alive in your consciousness. I would like to hold your attention by stretching out this book, recounting funny mishaps and little victories page after page, until we had a fat volume to put Tolstoy to shame. Would that I could describe for you the hero's troika with its fur robes and dashing horses! But this insidious disease is forcing me to draw back once again, to find other avenues of expression, for these fingers of mine are fumbling around like a smashed bag of hammers, and even though there are more stories to tell, the time will soon come when writing is more burden than pleasure. Yes, I am very grateful that a benevolent organization down in Toronto has offered to provide me with a new computer operated by a joy stick attached to the right arm of my wheelchair. But how can a toggle, no matter how agile, keep pace with my zigzagging mind?

Hopefully my tale contains a grain or two of wisdom. Perhaps it will inspire my fellow MS sufferers to make the most of their affliction with the time left. And may it persuade those able of limb to visit the lush isle of Sumatra, home of Gypsy Joe's Tripping Weed, where blissful pilgrims dispel the spiritual sclerosis that propels humanity towards an early grave.

Feel the love?